LIVING THINGS

LIVING THINGS

Fiona Robyn

Published by Lulu

Living Things
A Lulu book

Published in 2007 by Lulu.com
ISBN: 978-1-84799-127-0

Book design: Fiona Robyn
Cover design: Steve Pawinski

ACKNOWLEDGEMENTS

Grateful acknowledgements are made to the following publications and webzines where poems have appeared:

3rd muse: "Calling Kate" and "Mathilda"
Aesthetica: "Apples, pine, mint"
Black medina: "Blackbird" and "Eczema"
Conspire: "All of us"
Interpreters House: "Autumn" and "Living things"
Limestone: "Autumn" and "Love story"
nth position: "Circle line"
Obsessed with Pipework: "Schizophrenic"
Other Poetry: "Love story" and "Seeing William in a photo"
Poetry and Audience: "Red tree"
Poetry Kit: "Living things"
Poetry PF: "Therapy"
Rialto: "All of us", "Jam" and "Rock, Ballycastle"
Snakeskin: "Conker", "In Karen's bedroom" and "on ending a relationship"
Stirring: "Jam"
The sun always rises: "White Christmas"
this: "Seeing William in a photo"
Wandering Dog: "Snow"
Zuzu's Petals: "Rock, Ballycastle"

"Point of Change" was published as part of a pamphlet from Flarestack in 2005.

Affectionate thanks to Esther Morgan and Susan Utting for scrutinising this manuscript so carefully and for being so supportive over the years.

I've been lucky enough to learn much over the years at Moniza Alvi's class and at Arvon courses with Adrian Mitchell, Neil Rollinson, Selima Hill and Roddy Lumsden amongst others. Thank you to Neil Astley for taking the time to respond personally to my first ever attempt at poems.

Finally, gratitude and love to Steve for his help with the design of this book and for always encouraging me to do my thing.

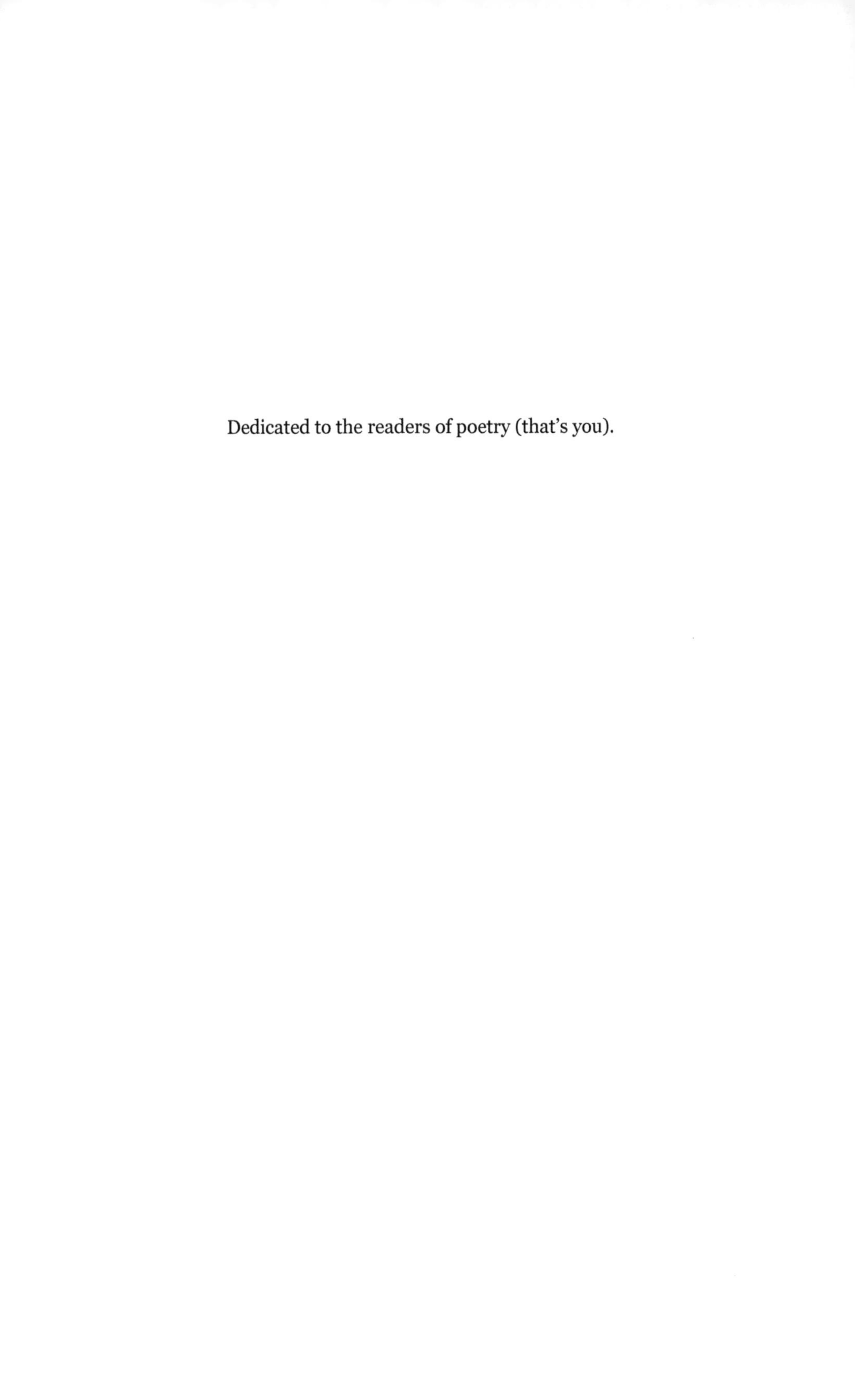

Dedicated to the readers of poetry (that's you).

CONTENTS

I had been my whole life a bell, and never knew it until
at that moment I was lifted and struck.

Annie Dillard

LIVING THINGS

I have carried living things in my hands all week, sneaked up on
daddy-long-legs, pulled them off painted walls and held their brittle bodies.
I've picked up blue-black beetles like shiny stones, moved them
from inside rooms to out; they stick to my thumb, they seem
happy enough to cling on. Best of all, the two young frogs
who'd come onto the kitchen tiles to see what they could find.
I watched them bending their tiny legs, toothpick bones inside,
felt their rubbery skin against mine as they pushed away, they were amazing.
I have held living things in my hands all week, knowing
if I wanted I could close the space between my fingers.
And I think how it might have been for those two frogs, to be lifted up
so high, so fast: when the light comes back they could be anywhere.

TORTOISESHELL CAT

He's lying at the side of the pavement
stretched out as if in front of a fire
half-wrapped in a sheet of plastic sacking.

Maybe someone used it to protect their hands
from death when they lifted him
from the tarmac and left him here.

His coat is rich oranges and browns
and he looks unharmed – no torn skin,
no limbs at unnatural angles.

I only know he's dead because his cheeks
are pulled back into a grimace, because
he doesn't flinch when I move up close.

I'd like to pick him up and take him home.
Soon after I watch a black cat stretch on a bright roof
absorbing sunshine through every strand of hair,
rolling over and over in ecstasy.

ROCK, BALLYCASTLE

Clear salt is growing on this rock,
or maybe the ocean's foamy fingers
stroked it on, or it banged and stuck
hurled by the purging wind.

Perhaps the rock sweated it out.
It won't dissolve on my tongue,
bent over with my hair blown back
the clacking of pebbles behind me.

THIMBLE JELLIES

A flock of mini pepper-pots
they float in cornflower blue
blowing kisses at the sky.

The red-brown cloud at their centres
is alive, hungry for the light
that has pierced the skin of the sea.

CALLING KATE

He decides to call it a day.
I hear about it not long after
they find his body.

I call Australia
where Kate is sleeping alone in a strange bed.
She is pleased to be woken by me,
presses the phone to her ear.

There are gaps in the line.

After I've told her
the holes in her voice get so big
I'm afraid I'll fall into them.

LOVE STORY

i

a year of nights in this room
music pumping like blood
passing the joint in ever smaller circles
talking the sun up

and now
the usual goodnight hug
stretching on like a motorway
the shock of your mouth
moving towards me
the beautiful clink
of teeth on teeth

ii

As it turns out, you don't love me.
I ask six men to put their cocks
inside me. After the sixth
I can still remember the colour
of my pale-pink skin against yours.

I don’t know how I got here.

I tie my hair around your wrists:
you drag me round behind you.

iii

After all this time,
you walk into my dream
like you own it.

I'm not surprised
that your eyes

swerve away
when you see me.

But then later on
as I stand in a field
looking at cows
your arms
are suddenly around me.

You see, I still
can't believe
you don't want me.

TELEPHONE COUNSELLING

In a quiet voice he tells me
his wife is dead. It was *sudden,*
horrible. She was *too young.*

We fumble around in the dark.
Everywhere he turns he slams
his face up against forever.

We speak for forty minutes
and afterwards I'm not sure how,
there was so little to say.

He hangs up to choose photos
of her smiling at parties,
to arrange them in albums.

I step outside quickly before
I break, sit on a cold iron step,
let water run onto my cheeks.

After a while I'm only
crying for myself. Dry my eyes.
Go back to the living.

ECZEMA

This morning my hands are covered in tiny bubbles.
They cluster around the base of my left thumb,
are on the palm-side of my fingers, each holding in

a drop of liquid wept from inside cells. I choose a fat one,
pinch it between my finger and thumb-nail, squeeze until
the wetness hits my cheek and taste the salt with the tip of my tongue.

It's begun. My heart bangs faster as I break the skin all over,
my hands are covered in dew. This popping, which is my only consolation,
fills the bubbles up with yellow pus and then the skin gets thick

and cracks appear, it hurts like hell, you can see the pink inside me.
Once I got to work and the blood splashed on my desk
and I had to go back and wipe it from the door where I came in.

And then the healing starts, the hard skin peels away, hangs off
like flakes of coconut, and underneath is purple, smooth, shining.
I carry my hands around and they are whole. They feel like neon.

BLACKBIRD

All night a blackbird sings outside my window.
I sleep for an hour and wake to the cat crying
at the door. There's morning light behind the curtains.
It's five a.m. and fifteen years ago.

I want to get up and walk to the lake with my friends,
stand around in the mist as the sun comes up
and go back to breakfast and lectures with something changed,
a knowledge that will mark us out from the others.

The light behind the curtains is a street lamp
and as the birdsong loops and coils towards me
I think of holding the day ahead. My days
are heavier now. Or something else is different.

HOW TO BE DAZZLED

Ask to be led
to a bluebell wood.
Sit, and once alone
feel the sun dapple you.
Take off your shoes.
Become quiet.

Become quiet, and listen
for the humming of the bluebells
clear and sweet as lollipops.
Now, open your eyes -

SNOW

I am thinking so hard about how I will describe
the exact feeling as it compacts under my feet

in shudders, I nearly forget to notice that the light
is more luminous than I have ever seen it

and that the young trees across the river
are as much white as they are black wood, and how

the froth on the chopped up water is filthy
against the white of fresh snow.

And how the empty sky, further away than usual
gives me more space to breathe.

ALDEBURGH BEACH

This morning the waves are restless.
Underneath them things are living out their lives.

Pebbles are piled up at the sea-edge
as if trickled from a huge hand.
Each one has its own genealogy,
a parent rock, a place it has travelled from.

The fine rain is almost horizontal.
I breathe it in, dissolve it into my blood.

The sea is happiest as froth, stretching out
its fingers, skipping faster, making shapes.
When it bangs itself onto the shore
it feels a release

as if moving its shoulder-blades diagonally
one way and then the other.

MATHILDA

Early morning. She bathes in
the cool shade of her stable,
regards me with faint curiosity.

I call to her
in a voice I think she will understand,
then try another. She is happy

where she is, she doesn't come to me
like the ponies who came to James Wright
in 'The Blessing', I can't skim her ears

with my fingertips, see if they are
delicate as the skin over a girl's wrist.
She turns her long nose away, maybe

to think of the neat thuds she leaves
in the grass as she gallops,
the fizz of sugar on her tongue.

SALEM

Crow-black and glinting,
he comes in from out there

tail straight up, a sweep for chimneys.
I give off circles of warmth.

He crawls to my neck
where blood beats close to the air.

I sniff in the fresh, cold smoke
clinging to his fur like burrs.

He tucks his head underneath my chin,
kneads my shoulder, is almost

inside me.
When he's drunk his fill he drops off

to lie stretched out, belly-up,
showing off teased out thistle-fluff fur,

ringletty, rusted to reddy-brown.
It hides nipples like baby button mushrooms.

I wipe gunge from sleepy eye-corners
drawing it out towards me

in a thin string that doesn't break.

AS THE TRAIN SLOWS AND STOPS

he lifts his head from his wife's shoulder.
One whole side of his face is deep hot pink,
the clay of his cheek has the basket-weave
pattern of her cardigan pressed into it.
He stretches his way out of sleep,
small noises escaping like moths.
His grown up family are amused.
He scolds them in Spanish, embarrassed,
they only laugh louder.

His wife sits quietly, her eyes full
of what they have forged between them
from a life-time of witnessing the best
and the worst in each other.

She holds him in a look of such love.

CIRCLE LINE

The pint he's cupped and savoured all afternoon
mixes with the chattering track and warm, used air.
He leans back, lets his eyes close and his mouth open.

There's a mug of sweet tea waiting for him at home,
and a grey dog called Charlie.
He dies quietly between Blackfriars and Temple.

It's fourteen hours before he's found.
He is thin under his clothes, the men who lift him
put too much strength into their arms.

SCHIZOPHRENIC

He's placing his foot as he would
a blown wren's egg into a girl's palm.
No-one is looking after his hair.

Wind time on a little faster:
the flower of his body unfurls
as people buzz past leaving smudges of colours
and plumes of breath like thrown away wings.

I want to go over and touch his shoulder
but I'm not sure if he'd turn,
snail-like, and wink
or go off in my face with a bang.

DOUGLAS BLACK

They wouldn't let me in, dahlin'. I tried.
The manager said they had to keep me out
because of all my diseases. Like the gangrene -
I've lost the tip of this finger already, see?
I need a tent, a stove, some cooking utensils.
My doctor gives me two or three years, sweetheart.
I'm not being funny. I need a tent, a stove.
I'm not a piece of shit on the street, dahlin',
I'm a human being. Will you pass on a message?
Tell him I came about the letter, he'll know me:
Douglas Black. I need some cooking utensils.
They wouldn't let me in, dahlin'. I tried.

WAITING FOR A TRAIN, CARLISLE

His black knitted hat is pulled down tight,
his face is squashed and red. He rolls his head
from side to side, drawing figures of eight with his crown.

When he pauses he lets out whistles: short bird-calls,
pure, sliding bursts of sound. There's an answer
from somewhere in this cold, cavernous space, the same tune

or a variation. Maybe it's the huddle of train-spotters
at the end of the platform across the tracks
recognising something of themselves in the music.

ARE YOU OUT THERE DARREN BUFFIN?

At first I think he has straw in his hair
but looking closer I see that
the layer of plastic colour has weakened,
split, let the white card show through
as patches of lightening.

They've been taking this photo out
for thirteen years now, touching his face
with the tips of their thumbs.

THE POINT OF CHANGE

Kate

My world is turning sour.
The postman has been reading my letters.
My husband smells of other women.
The children leave toys on the stairs to trip me up.

Today at breakfast
I returned to the table and noticed
my orange juice had been moved.
I looked at their faces carefully,
tipped it down the sink –

Ian

In my room I have
a cuddly giraffe and
a blue jug and
a special comb to brush my beard.

Then my jug broke.
I cried because
the ladies would be angry.

Then I got sellotape and
wrapped it round and round.
It took ages.

Then a lady came and
they all came in
pointing and laughing.

I like people laughing like
mummy when I dance for her but

this laughing was different –

Charley

from behind the paper
I listen to the
all-day squabbling

when one of them trips
falls on its head
and after a pause
squeals
like a washing machine on full spin

I pick it up
draw back my hand

and look down into
my own face
the day I knocked
the pie from the table

and stop my hand
mid-air,
my son dangling –

Eddie

She has a moustache
and comes round twice weekly
to iron my shirts.

Today she looks up
with a twinkle in her eyes.
I smile

noticing for the first time
her beautiful eyelashes –

Bea

Kept it safe,
that pale blue egg
freckled like my father.
Filled a shoe-box
with tissue
torn to confetti.
Cupped it until
blood-warm
twice daily.

Different this time,
this flesh-clot
twisting inside me
impatient for
a mouthful of milk.
Not made
of chocolate
this time.
I want it out
and quiet –

Gordon

When he first told me I gagged.
Three years have passed. Now they have
a house together, a life.
My wife visits them alone.
Still when I close my eyes I see
the naked horror of them together.

Often my wife brings home news.
I fake indifference. Then she brings
the first sweet honey from bees
they keep in wooden hives.
It was the best I'd ever tasted.
I spread it on my toast for breakfast.

Each morning I think of my son.
The size of my love. When I scrape
the last of it from the bottom
of the pot I drive to their house.
A young man comes to answer the door.
He shakes my hand and asks me in –

Oliver

We sit in awkward silence
side by side on the sofa.
I'm thinking I'm too old for all this

when my dead wife appears
perched on the television.
She gives me the thumbs up

so I reach across
and click off the lamp
to see what will happen.

Fingertips like cobwebs
land on my inside arm,
travel up and down –

THE BATHWATER IS GOLDEN, SMELLS OF FLOWERS

The bathwater is golden, smells of flowers.
Light flickers on the curves of mini-waves

and through the yellow haze my skin is pale.
I'd rather see the colours underneath,

I want to get to know my insides better.
Are livers brown or purple? Does the fat

around my heart look creamy? Does it glisten?
How close to orange is freshly filtered blood?

Are bones as white as rice or stained like teeth?
Could lungs be soft pink wings if opened out?

One day, when my time is nearly up
maybe I'll try it. Let out a cloud of red.

HAIR

There was a seizure – she shook her husband awake.
Now she lies on this bed, won't open her eyes.

Her husband sits beside her, thinks of the cancer.
Every day there is more of her hair on her pillow.

The roots of it are slipping from their sockets
as she lets out each breath. There. There.

ON ENDING A RELATIONSHIP

I know that I must do it
as quickly and painlessly as possible

like the old poet who recommended scissors
as the best way of disposing of
newly born kittens

CAMP SUNBURST

Look inside these children -
hold them up to the light
like beach-washed glass.

There are black crystals forming
in the luminous red of their blood.
It's not looking good for them.

Watch them here in this bright space.
They touch each other whenever they can,
the laughter pours out of them.

RED TREE

In October it cracks open like an egg,
becomes the colour of fights, of lips
men would kill to kiss.

The leaves are lit up from within
and bursting with banquets,
chandeliers, all-night dancing.
Unable to bear their own brightness

they let go of their twigs too soon.
The tree can hardly wait to be red again.

COW SISTER

The train mutters
to itself, no-one listens.
Looking out, her eyes are full
of early morning mist.

Every time she passes a cow
she dips her head
in silent acknowledgement.
She belongs with grass.

HERON

Nearly Christmas.
The usual Thursday
morning ritual:

a hot breakfast, orange
and raspberry juice,
window seat in Starbucks.

These scraps of paper
covered in words trying
to become poems.

And then your text:
"Stop writing and
send me a kiss".

It lands like a heron.
The words scatter,
find their places.

SEEING WILLIAM IN A PHOTO

brings it back like birds exploding
from the tops of forests.
The blanket heat of Sarawak.
His dirt-brown skin, French accent.

We were too young to know about sex.
We curled up like cubs
in the grass behind the squash courts.

IN KAREN'S BEDROOM

Our straight brown bodies
changing, new fat
cuddling our bones,
we locked ourselves in

and slipped into her mum's
negligee, the cold silk
licking our skin.
We took turns to move

for each other - showing
flashes of breast and
glimpses of bum.
We were blooming and knew it.

JAM

I was asked to put my lips around the tube
that pistoned jam into the hearts of do-nuts.

He had been there longer than any of us,
he knew about bread. He tried his luck

asking every Saturday for a kiss –
he'd only slide his tongue inside my mouth

for a second. I wasn't ready
but I liked his eyes on me as I stood

at the sink and sucked, sucked so hard my cheeks
ached from the effort, thick gluey jam

suddenly sweet in my mouth. I waited
a second, maybe two. Spat it out.

BLUE SILK PYJAMAS

They sit in a crumpled pile where they are dropped
waiting to be wrapped in paper scattered with snow-flakes.
Between the electric white and the deep black of the folds
are all of the blues you'd find in a winter sea.
They catch and hold the light
as if they are a sculpture in steel,
the kind you long to skim your fingertips over.

They're a present for my grandma,
and while I hope she'll luxuriate in their silkiness
I fear instead that they'll go the same way
as the present I bought her last year,
a translucent black shawl
embroidered with jewelled peacock whorls
that was too fancy, too cold.

ON BEING HALF OF A PAIR

I am learning it again
from the beginning:
how to be alone

as I look out through glass
at strings of beads shining in the dark

as headlights swing round towards me
car after car not containing him

and I am trying
to learn it again

(waiting like a dog)

how to be alone

ALL OF US

Last night a friend read
my poems
for the first time
and praised several before
picking up her magazine again.
I wanted her to read
everything I
had ever written.

All of us whispering listen, listen, listen.

THERAPY

When I think of my clients at odd moments during the day
when turning the car into our road or looking up at a flat sky
it is mostly their sadness, not their anger or joy, that rushes into me
like a loaded water-colour brush dipped onto paper.

This is because the instrument inside me that recognises sadness
is fine-tuned after years of practising on my parents. This part of me
lows like a cow for its calf. This part of me lows like a cow for its calf.

APPLES, PINE, MINT

I snap my neck to see what hit my head.
It's shining in the dirt; a perfect leaf,
the size of a dinner-plate. A few steps on
it pulls me back. I bend and pick it up,
hold it at the end of the long stem.
It moves along beside me like a wing.
When I get to where I'm going to
I fold it up and slip it into my bag.

The next day I drive to a strange place
to meet a strange man in a grand hotel.
Afterwards the space inside my car
is filled with scent: apples, pine, mint.
I dig around and find my folded leaf,
shrunken, brown, it doesn't want to open
out, it cracks and splits. I wind the window,
throw it onto the soil and I am happy.

KATE AT TWENTY-NINE

The older I get, the more
that details move me.

New leaves on my orange
tree. Fresh mint

crushed and stirred in mojito.
As she speaks

the words catch in her throat,
they are so sweet.

CONKER

I choose the shiniest, let the others be.
It fits inside my fist as perfectly

as a foetus fits inside its mother.
The skin's a rich and glossed mahogany,

the base a paper-bag brown smeared with white.
It's cool against my cheek and smooth as ice.

I'd like to place it on my tongue and suck
so I don't have to waste my breath on talk.

LESS CARELESS

A small black swelling held onto the tip of that twig for weeks.
I watched it from my bus as the cleaning ladies shuffled off

and the office workers let them pass, imagined it to be full of sticky fluid
or maybe even grubs, growing sleeker by the day, but green came out of it.

This happened to trees all along my route to work – green commas
all over them, opening up, taking in food from the air.

They basked in the sun all Summer, these leaves, breezes curving
their stems, I was less careless this year, I paid attention.

WRITING ON THE BEACH, WRABNESS

The boats all nod, good morning Fiona, good morning.
The pebbles rattle. A single blackbird sings.

The edges of my body blossom into goose-pimples.
I carry a chair towards the edge of the water.

I start to write – line after line of clear words.
The pages are lit in turn by the lemon sun, the pointed stars.

Notebooks fill up as the tide breathes in and out.
Birds come and go. My hair and nails grow longer.

Every so often honeyed phrases appear from nowhere.
I weep at the light of them, the truth of them.

When I'm withered it lands on the page like a hummingbird:
the perfect sentence. The shock of it kills me.

Men lift my bones into a boat, pitch me into the sea.
My notebooks are piled up high and burn in a bonfire.

People come from far away to hold their arms out straight
and spread their fingers. My words keep them warm.

WHITE CHRISTMAS

I choose a sheet by touch.
She folds it in two
and still it is bigger than me.

Out where it's slippery
the wind has picked up,
I hold the card close to my chest.

I'll cut it into angel-shapes,
sprinkled with dust the colour of sun on snow.
They'll fly to the people I love
who'll tilt them and catch sparkles in their eyes.

I feel a tickling like tiny silver spiders.
The length of the fold sinks in through my skin
to fuse with my spine; blood pumps to the tips.
I step up. Cold air rosies my cheeks,
stars catch in my hair.

I'm zooming towards the tallest pine
in all of Canada.

A KIND OF APOLOGY

I climb over the fence and walk towards them.
I want to touch their rubbery noses
but I'm also showing off – I'm fourteen, and cocky.
I moo, offer plucked grass from a flat palm.
A red one notices first and trundles over; soon
they're all on the move, a swarm of curious cows.

The black one is running now, it's a bullock,
it gets bigger and bigger. I stumble backwards
over hard clods of earth, panic blooming in my chest.
One of them catches me with a sharp horn
before I jump back over the fence to safety.
Mum opens her arms, and dad is laughing.

Fifteen years later he remembers the shock
of seeing those huge beasts running at his daughter.
He laughed because he didn't know what else to do,
because he was scared. It is a kind of apology,
for laughing and for all the other things.
He was doing his best, we are all of us doing our best.

AUTUMN

It is cold. I sit in the centre of a circle of nuns. They are lying
under the grass, their heads or feet pointing towards me.

Each sister is marked with a stump of stone. A silver plaque
shows her name, how long she had, when she was taken by God.

Off to the left are trees, and to my right four fat pheasants
are wandering around the convent gardens. Further away

the hills are under mist. I think a fire is gently crackling
somewhere hidden in the trees until I turn and really listen.

It is the orangey leaves – they are glancing off each other
as they fall, snapping, pattering and landing with a whisper.

There are four more stones a little way from the others.
Here, holes were dug for Annie, Irene, Frances and Joan,

all of them children. Sister Elizabeth had ninety-six
chances to hear this burning. Annie had ninety less.

Fiona Robyn is the author of 'A Year of Questions: How to slow down and fall in love with life'. She also writes fiction. She writes regular blogs at www.asmallstone.com and www.lovethequestions.com and her website is at www.fionarobyn.com. She lives in Hampshire with her partner, cats and vegetable patch. This is her first collection of poems.

www.ingramcontent.com/pod-product-compliance
Ingram Content Group UK Ltd.
Pitfield, Milton Keynes, MK11 3LW, UK
UKHW041914190726
13854UKWH00003B/1248